To my mother, Frances Shapiro —LS

To Kyoko Yoshida —HT

It's Time to Sleep in Your Own Bed

Lawrence E. Shapiro, Ph.D.
Illustrated by **Hideko Takahashi**

Instant Help Books

Alex slept with his mommy
and daddy every night.

He loved to snuggle
with Mommy.

In the morning, he loved to play airplane with Daddy.

Sometimes Alex and Daddy hid under the covers and waited for Mommy to find them.

Then one day Mommy said to Alex, "Tonight you get to sleep all by yourself."

But Alex didn't want to sleep all by himself.

"You're a big boy now, and it's time to sleep in your very own bed," said Mommy.

Later that day, Alex's new bed arrived.

Mommy covered it with new
sheets and a soft blanket.
Daddy tucked in Alex's bear.

Alex liked playing on his new bed very much.

But he didn't want to sleep in it!

That night, after Alex got ready
for bed, Mommy and Daddy
came to tuck him in.

They read Alex his favorite story. Then they kissed him good night and left the room.

Alex snuggled with his bear,
but it wasn't the same as
snuggling with Mommy.

Alex played airplane, but it wasn't as fun as playing airplane with Daddy.

Alex didn't like sleeping alone in his own bed. He wanted to sleep with Mommy and Daddy.

"Mommy! Daddy! I want to sleep with you," cried Alex.

"You're a big boy now, and big boys sleep in their own beds," Mommy and Daddy said gently.

"I love you," said Mommy.
"I love you," said Daddy.
"I love you, too," said Alex.

Alex closed his eyes and
hugged his bear tight.

He wanted to call out again
for Mommy and Daddy . . .
but he didn't.

He wanted to crawl into their
bed . . . but he didn't. Instead,
Alex fell asleep.

When Alex woke up, Mommy and Daddy said, "We're so proud of you, Alex. You slept all alone in your own bed!"

Then Mommy and Daddy gave Alex a special award.

You did it!
You slept in
your own bed!
Hugs and Kisses, Mommy and Daddy

Advice for Parents

Dear Parents,

Many parents like to have their children sleep with them when they are infants. It helps them bond with their children, and it is certainly easier for nighttime feedings, particularly for nursing. But there comes a time when all children need to sleep in their own beds, and this transition can be a difficult experience that parents dread . . . and avoid.

My own feeling is that children should make the transition to sleeping in their own beds between the ages of twelve and eighteen months. By this age, children are bonded to their parents, and their need for independence outweighs their need for nighttime closeness. If you wait beyond this age (as you may already have), it will be easier for children to climb out of their crib or bed and back into yours.

Many parents wait too long to make a rule that kids must sleep in their own beds. I have talked to parents with children who are three, five, seven years old and even older, who still sleep in their parents' bed. These parents tell me that their kids thrash around and keep them up at night; that having their kids in their bed has caused arguments with their spouse; and that they want their children to sleep in their own beds, but that they are too tired at night to fight about it.

It is my hope that reading this book with your young child will help ease your child's transition out of your bed and into his or her own.

Here are some things that happen in the story that you can do, too:

1. **Prepare your child for the day that he will begin to sleep in his own bed, but not too far in advance.**
2. **Make your child's bed a special place. Pick out sheets and blankets that your child likes. Perhaps get a new stuffed animal that has particular meaning to your child, like a lion to guard him in the night, or a very soft bear to hug.**

3. Emphasize that all big kids sleep in their own beds, and praise your child for being so grown up.

4. Once you have your child sleep in his own bed, do not give in to protest. Keep emphasizing that he is a big kid now, and that big kids sleep in their own beds.

5. Do not give in! If you are consistent, the complaining will stop in a few days. If you give in, the complaining will last weeks, months, or longer.

6. The morning after the first night that your child sleeps in his own bed, give him a certificate, like the one in the story. You can print out a certificate from our website, www.TransitionTimesBooks.com. Hang it over his bed to tell the world about his accomplishment.

If your child is still giving you a hard time about sleeping in his own bed, there are other things you can do:

1. Sleep next to your child's bed on the first night, and move a little farther away each successive night.

2. Start a sticker program, and give your child a sticker every night he sleeps in his own bed without a fuss.

3. Talk to older children about the importance of privacy, as well as the importance of a good night's sleep. Children who grow up sleeping in a family bed might need to be taught ways to fall asleep by themselves. Some ways to teach your child to fall asleep by himself include: muscle relaxation and deep breathing practice, using imagery to stop worry and anxiety, removing distractions from the room (such as cell phones and computers, which tempt children to avoid sleep).

4. Examine your parenting style and how you set limits. When you set clear limits about every aspect of your child's life, bedtime battles will soon go away. See our website for more recommended tips.

Many aspects of parenting are difficult, and getting a child to sleep in his own bed is one that many parents struggle with. It may help to remember that there will be many transition times in your child's life, and when you handle them with confidence and a positive attitude, both you and your child will benefit.

Good luck!

Lawrence Shapiro, Ph.D.

The **transition times** series is designed to help parents understand the importance of addressing developmental issues at the right time and in the right way. Each book addresses a specific transition in the lives of children, when they often need a gentle nudge forward on the road to responsibility and independence. The books provide parents with a way to talk to their children that will hold their interest and make facing life's challenges seem less overwhelming. The books also help parents understand age-appropriate expectations, and give them a simple and clear context to set realistic limits. Reading the books to children will make bumpy transition times just a little bit smoother.

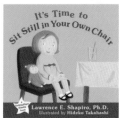

Publisher's Note

This publication is sold with the understanding that the publisher is not engaged in rendering psychological or other professional services. If expert assistance or counseling is needed, the services of a competent professional should be sought.

An Instant Help Book

Distributed in Canada by Raincoast Books

Text copyright © 2008 by Lawrence Shapiro, Ph.D.
New Harbinger Publications, Inc.
5674 Shattuck Avenue
Oakland, CA 94609
www.newharbinger.com

Illustrations by Hideko Takahashi
Cover and text design by Amy Shoup
Acquired by Tesilya Hanauer
The illustrations were done in acrylic paint on multimedia paper.
This book was typeset in Souvenir BT.

Library of Congress Cataloging-in-Publication Data
Shapiro, Lawrence E.
  It's time to sleep in your own bed : a transition time book / Lawrence E. Shapiro.
    p. cm. -- (Transition times)
  ISBN-13: 978-1-57224-586-0 (hardcover : alk. paper)
  ISBN-10: 1-57224-586-7 (hardcover : alk. paper) 1. Co-sleeping. 2. Infants--Sleep. 3. Children--Sleep. I. Title.
  GT3000.5.C67S527 2008
  649'.122--dc22

                              2008029591

All Rights Reserved
Printed in Thailand

10   09   08

10   9   8   7   6   5   4   3   2   1

First printing